P9-AOI-077

ERICH FUCHS

Journey to the Moon

A Seymour Lawrence Book
Delacorte Press / New York

Originally published in Germany by Heinrich Ellermann, München under the title HIER APOLLO 11.
© 1969 by Verlag Heinrich Ellermann, München. English translation Copyright © 1969 by
Abelard-Schumann Ltd. All rights reserved. No part of this book may be reproduced in
any form or by any means without the prior written permission of the Publisher, excepting
brief quotes used in connection with reviews written specifically for inclusion in a
magazine or newspaper.
Library of Congress Catalog Card Number: 74-103151
Manufactured in Germany. First American Printing.

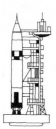

July 16, 1969. On the launching pad at Cape Kennedy stands a rocket 363 feet high. At the top is the spacecraft *Apollo 11*. Inside are the three astronauts: Neil Armstrong, Edwin Aldrin, and Michael Collins. They are waiting for the signal to start their flight to the Moon. Many people are waiting with them. They have come to Cape Kennedy from all over the world.

10—9—8—7—6—5—4—3—2—1—lift off! With a great roar the rocket rises, slowly at first, then faster and faster, away from the Earth and all the people.

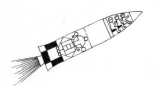

The rocket is made up of three sections, or stages. The first two stages take the spacecraft away from the Earth and are left behind as soon as their fuel tanks are empty. The third stage, which carries *Apollo 11*, takes the spacecraft first into an orbit around the Earth and then in the direction of the Moon.

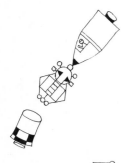

On the way to the Moon the command ship, named *Columbia*, separates from the third stage of the rocket. The astronauts turn the *Columbia* around, return to the rocket, join up with it, and then pull the Moon-landing craft, named *Eagle*, away. The third stage of the rocket is also left to drift in space.

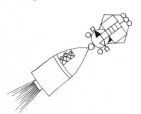

Joined together, the *Columbia* and the *Eagle* travel toward the Moon. The astronauts report to the Mission Control Station in Texas by radio. All the instruments and systems are working properly. After a three-day flight, the *Columbia* slows down and goes into orbit around the Moon.

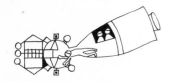

After circling the Moon several times, Armstrong and Aldrin crawl from the *Columbia* into the *Eagle*. The *Eagle* and the *Columbia* separate. Collins, now alone, circles the Moon in the command ship *Columbia*.

After carefully checking their instruments Armstrong and Aldrin start going down toward the Moon. Slowly the *Eagle* sinks to the surface. Armstrong steers past craters and boulders until he finds a flat plain. The long legs of the landing craft touch the surface. The *Eagle* has landed.

c
629.45
F951j

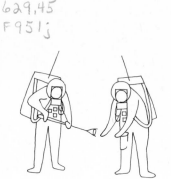

July 21. Neil Armstrong opens the hatch of the *Eagle* and climbs slowly down the ladder. His foot touches the ground. He is the first man to step on the Moon. "One small step for a man, but one giant leap for mankind," he says. Edwin Aldrin soon follows him. They put up scientific instruments, as well as the flag of the United States. They take photographs and television pictures and collect samples of rock. They walk on the Moon for more than two hours.

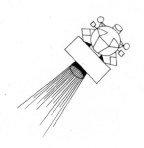

Now Armstrong and Aldrin must return to the command ship *Columbia*, in which Collins still circles the Moon. The upper part of the *Eagle*, with the two astronauts inside, fires a rocket to lift itself from the Moon. The lower part remains on the Moon, bearing a plaque with these words: "We came in peace for all mankind." The astronauts reach the *Columbia* and link up with it. They crawl back into the command ship, carrying the rock samples from the Moon.

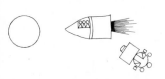

The rocket motor in the *Columbia* is fired to speed the three astronauts on their way home to Earth. The *Eagle* is left behind to circle the Moon. The closer the astronauts come to Earth, the larger it looks.

Three days after leaving the Moon, *Apollo 11*, now only a small capsule, plunges into the Earth's atmosphere. Three parachutes are released, carrying the capsule gently downward.

July 24. *Apollo 11* splashes down in the Pacific Ocean. Helicopters from the aircraft carrier *Hornet* hover over it. Frogmen jump into the water and place a floating collar around the capsule to keep it from sinking, and the hatch is opened. The astronauts climb out into a rubber dinghy. From there they are hoisted into the helicopter *Navy 66* and taken to the aircraft carrier. Other helicopters pick up the capsule. The eight-day journey to the Moon is over.

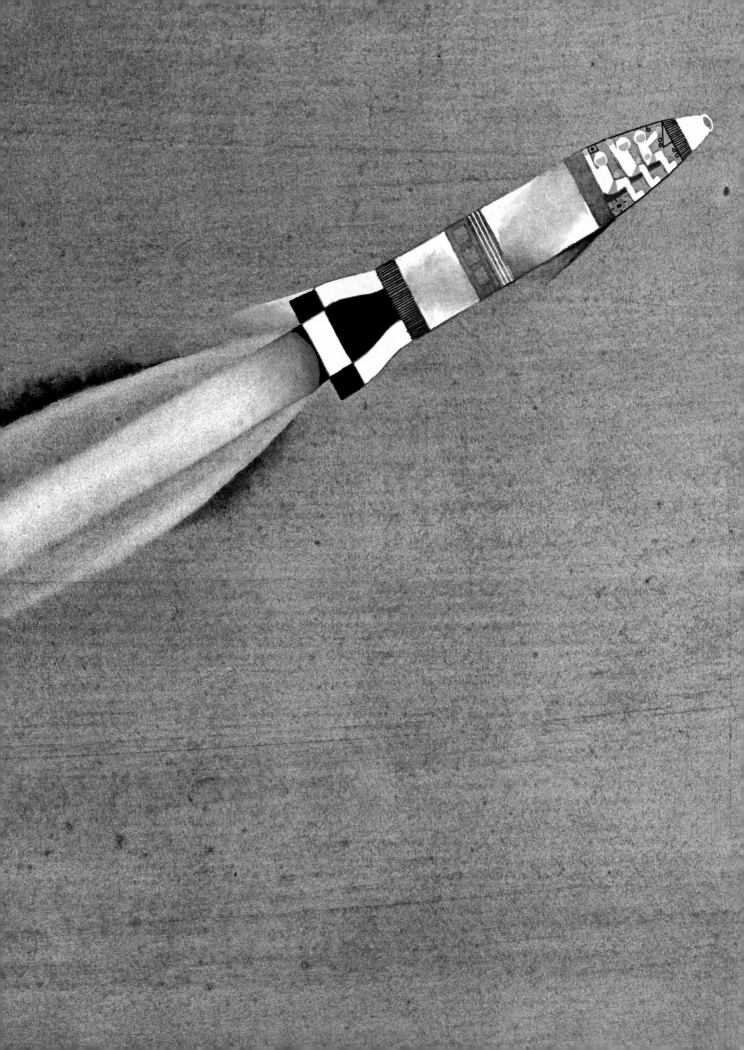

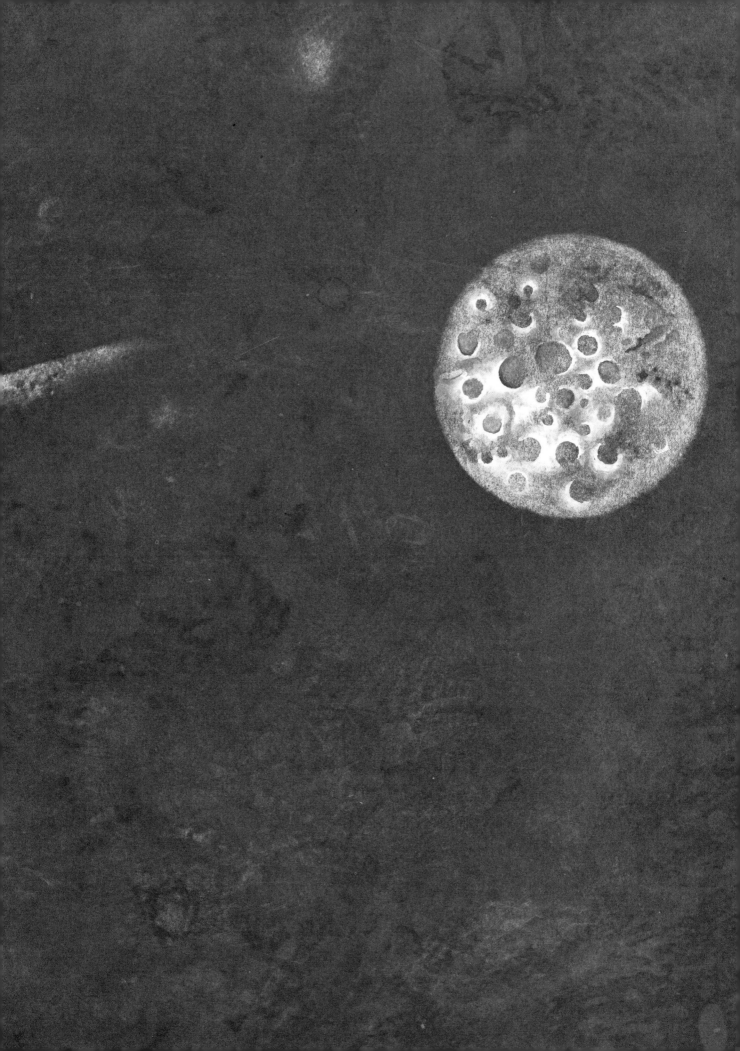

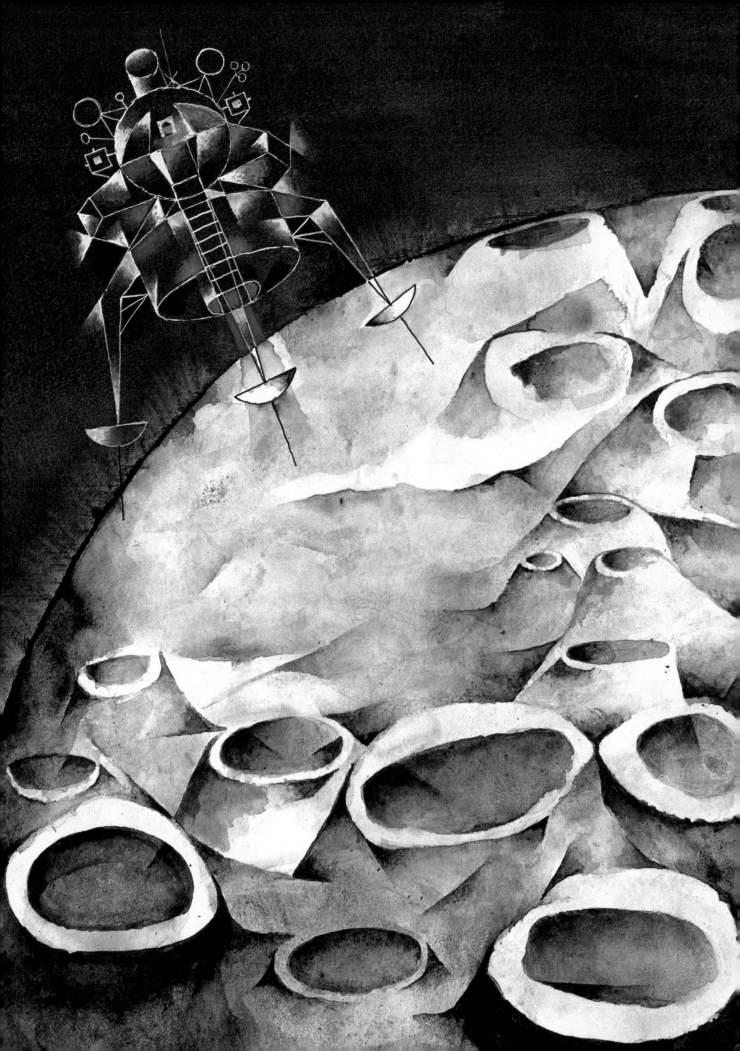

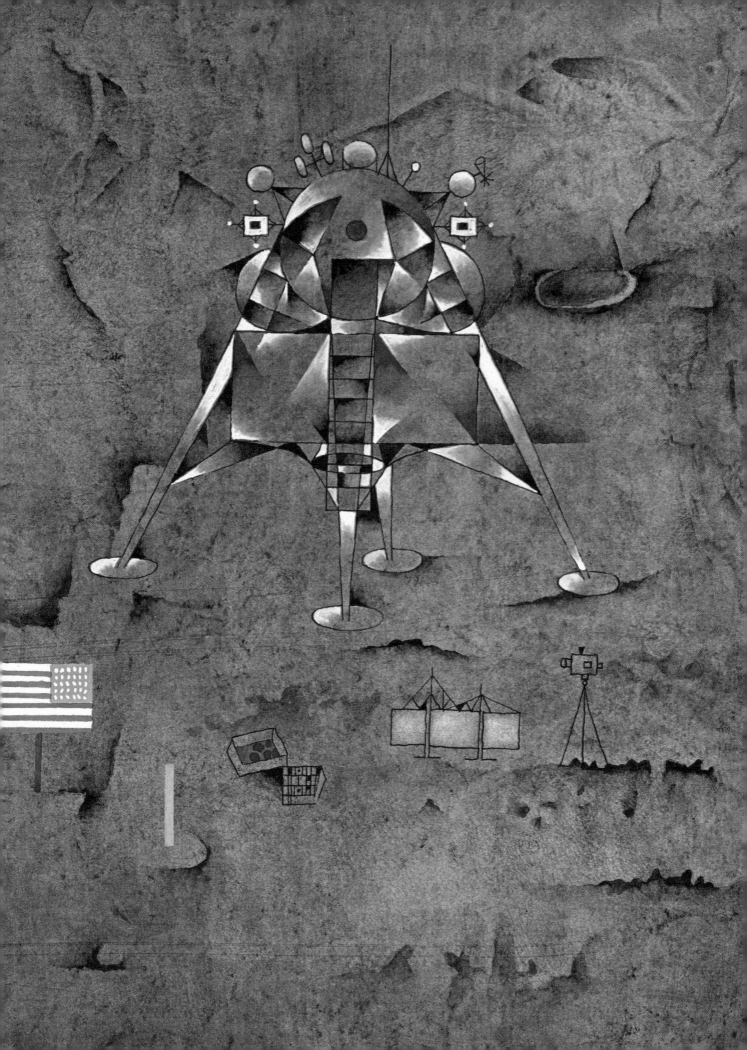

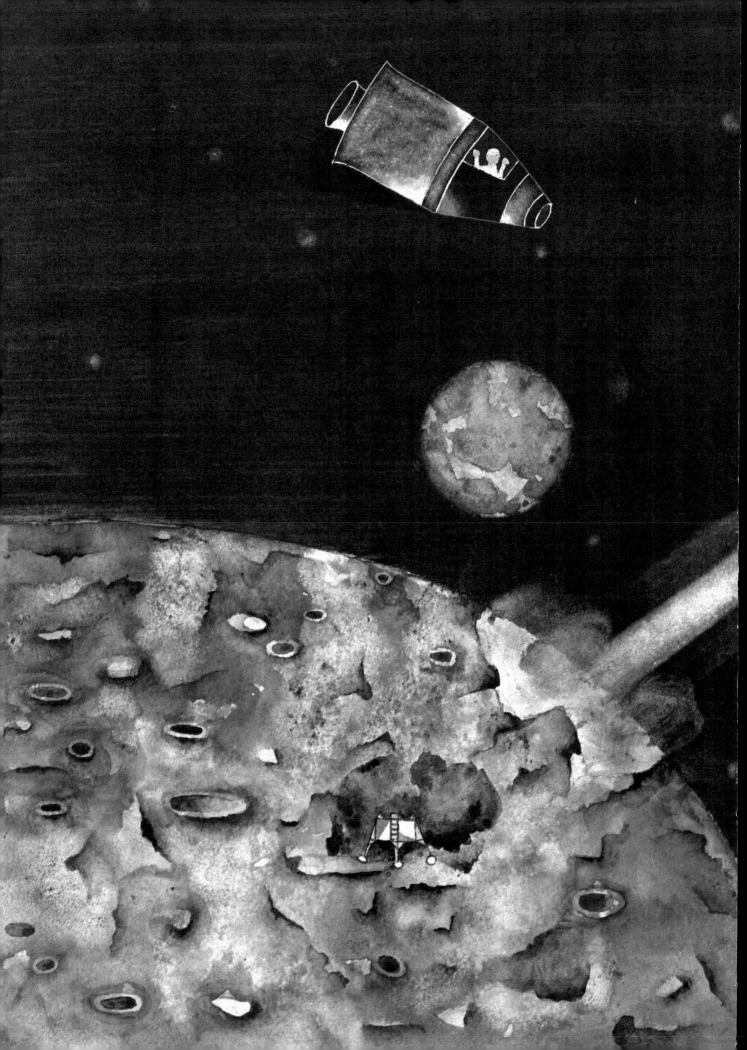

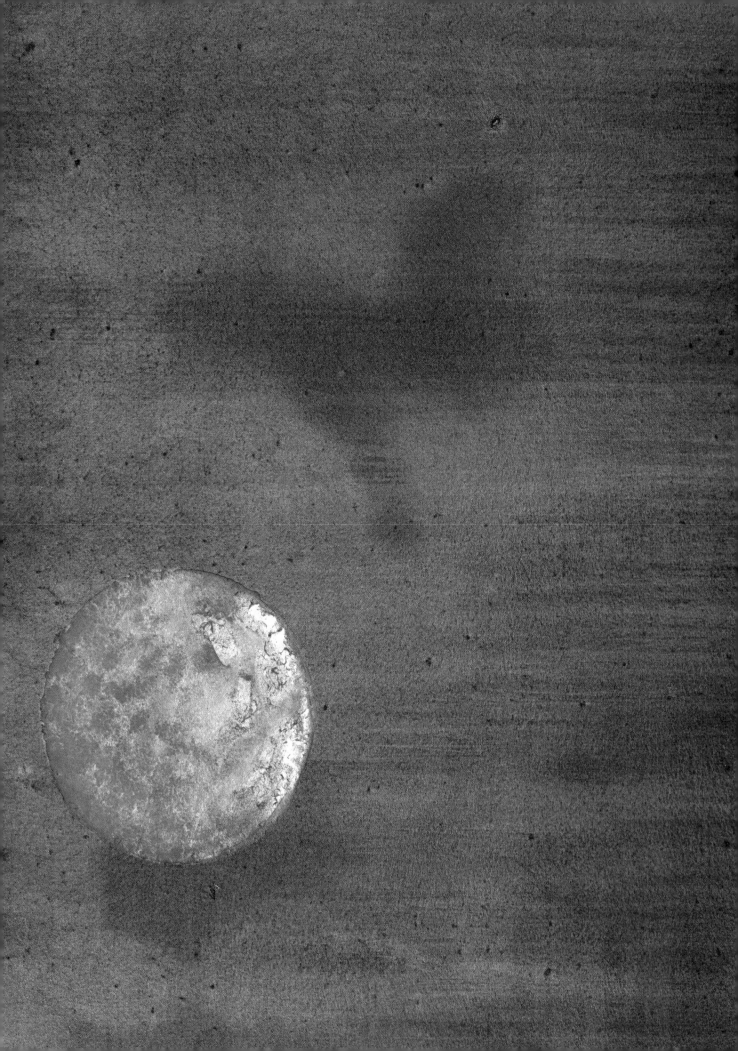

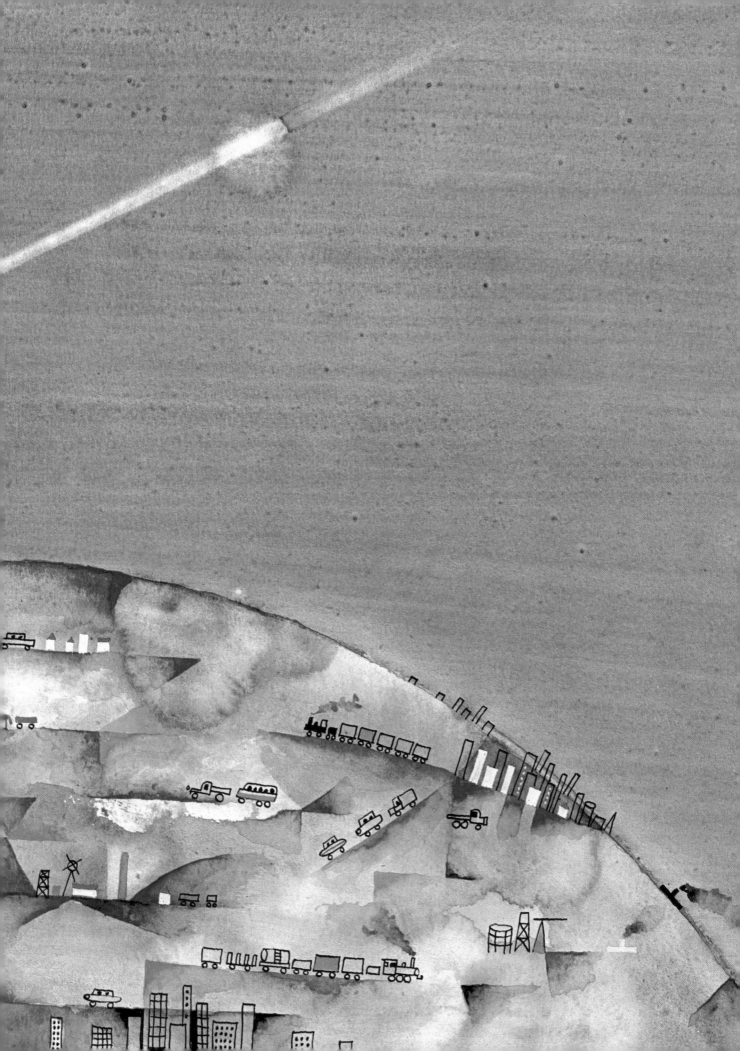